FIND
THE
CAT AND MORE!

Prepositions
Volume 1

Written and Photographed
by
Cindy Olejar

This book was printed in the United States of America.

ISBN-13: 978-1500744649 .
ISBN-10: 1500744646

All photos were taken by the author.

To contact the author email Cindy Olejar at:
findthecatandmore@yahoo.com

To order additional copies of this book go to:
www.findthecatandmore.com

This book is dedicated to Louie the cat. He loved to watch animal videos, snuggle, play with scarves, eat wet food, and get petted.

One of the intentions when reading this book is to practice using prepositions to say where the cat is located compared to the other objects in the photos. You can also come up with other sentences to find the cat that are not in this book.

Examples of some prepositions:
above, across, against, along, among, around, at, behind, below, beneath, beside, between, beyond, by, close to, in, in front of, left of, near, next to, on, over, right of, through, to, toward, under, upon, within

You can also find other objects in the photos and give clues using prepositions to have someone find the object.

To get a free lesson plan for this book go to 'How To Use The Books' at:
www.findthecatandmore.com

Have fun and be creative!

Where is the cat?

The cat is **near** the front door.

The cat is **against** the post.

The cat is **on** the porch.

Where is the cat?

The cat is **above** a bush.

The cat is **below** the roof.

The cat is **close to** the railing.

Where is the cat?

The cat is **in** the shade.

The cat is **on** a hill.

The cat is **among** the flowers.

Where is the cat?

The cat is **right of** a window.

The cat is **left of** a fence.

The cat is **near** the door.

Where is the cat?

The cat is **below** a window.

The cat is **between** two trees.

Where is the cat?

The cat is **near** the porch.

The cat is **beyond** the steps.

The cat is **on** the ledge.

Where is the cat?

The cat is **near** a window.

The cat is **beyond** the recycle bin.

The cat is **on** a top step.

Where is the cat?

The cat is **in** the shade.

The cat is **among** the grass and flowers.

Where is the cat?

The cat is **left of** a tree.

The cat is **below** the roof.

The cat is **on** the chair.

Where is the cat?

The cat is **above** the ground.

The cat is **on** the windowsill.

The cat is **behind** the curtain.

Where is the cat?

The cat is **in front of** the garage.

The cat is **near** the recycle bin.

The cat is **on** the picnic table.

Where is the cat?

The cat is **between** the house and the dirt pile.

The cat's head is sticking **above** the grass.

Where is the cat?

The cat is **above** the floor.

The cat is **near** the stage.

The cat is **on** a chair.

Where is the cat?

The cat is **near** a window.

The cat is **beyond** the table.

The cat is **on** top of a couch.

Where is the cat?

The cat is **beneath** a truck.

The cat is **next to** a tire.

Where is the cat?

The cat is **next to** a tree.

The cat is **near** a step.

The cat is **close to** a railing.

Where is the cat?

The cat is **next to** the grass.

The cat is **on** the cement.

The cat is **under** the railing.

Where is the cat?

The cat is **near** the step.

The cat is **on** some bark.

The cat is **under** the leaves.

Where is the cat?

The cat is **near** the mirror.

The cat is **in front of** the curtain.

The cat is **on top of** the black box.

Where is the cat?

The cat is **beyond** the barbeque.

The cat is **right of** the oar.

Where is the cat?

Fill in the blank with the prepositional words that fit the photo.

The cat is _____the porch.

The cat is _____ the steps.

The cat is _____
_____.

Where is the cat?

The cat is _____ the floor.

The cat is _____ the fireplace.

The cat is _____ _____.

Where is the cat?

The cat is _____ the ledge.

The cat is _____ the steps.

The cat is _____
_____.

Paste your own cat photo below from a magazine or newspaper or draw a picture of a cat hiding somewhere. Then write a sentence or two saying where the cat is located using prepositions.

_____

_____

I hope you had fun finding the cat and more.
Take a walk today and see if you can find any cats.
Meow!

These are other books written by this author that work
on nouns, verbs, prepositions, adjectives and adverbs.
Check them out at:

findthecatandmore.com

Describe the Cat!
Describe the Dog!
Find the Cat and More! Volume 2
Find the Cat and More! Volume 3
How is the Cat Acting?
How is the Dog Acting?
What Does the Cat See?
What is the Dog Doing?
What are the Dogs Doing?
When Does the Cat Eat, Sleep, Play and More?
Where is the Dog?

Cindy Olejar lives in
Seattle, WA.
findthecatandmore@yahoo.com
www.findthecatandmore.com

THE END!

Made in the USA
Columbia, SC
21 June 2023